The Empathic Parent's Guide to Raising an Anxious Child

How to Help Your Kids Overcome Shyness, Worry, Separation and Social Anxiety

Freeda Meighan

Copyright © 2020 by Freeda Meighan

All rights reserved.

The content contained within this book may not be reproduced, duplicated or transmitted without direct written permission from the author or the publisher. Under no circumstances will any blame or legal responsibility be held against the publisher, or author, for any damages, reparation, or monetary loss due to the information contained within this book. Either directly or indirectly. You are responsible for your own choices, actions, and results.

Legal Notice:

This book is copyright protected. This book is only for personal use. You cannot amend, distribute, sell, use, quote or paraphrase any part, or the content within this book, without the consent of the author or publisher.

Disclaimer Notice:

Please note the information contained within this document is for educational and entertainment purposes only. All effort has been executed to present accurate, up to date, and reliable, complete information. No warranties of any kind are declared or implied. Readers acknowledge that the author is not engaging in the rendering of legal, financial, medical or professional advice. The content within this book has been derived from various sources. Please consult a licensed professional before attempting any techniques outlined in this book. By reading this document, the reader agrees that under no circumstances is the author responsible for any losses, direct or indirect, which are incurred as a result of the use of the information contained within this document, including, but not limited to, — errors, omissions, or inaccuracies.

Join Our Support Group

Finding a supportive community can be hard. Many parents feel like they are alone in their parenting struggles and that no one understands what it is like to raise children today. In order to make the most of your time and get more out of this book, I highly encourage you to join our active community on Facebook.

Don't be afraid to reach out. You're never alone in this journey, and these are excellent resources that can support you.

See you there,

Freeda Meighan

JOIN NOW

https://bit.ly/3zulOsI

FREE EBOOK

SIGN UP TO MY MAILING LIST TO GET A FREE EBOOK

More freebies...

 Receive weekly parenting tips.
 Get advance readers' copy of my books for FREE!
 Get a chance to download audiobooks for FREE!
 Get a chance to win paperback giveaways.
And more!

WWW.FREEDAMEIGHAN.COM

Contents

Introduction	1
Chapter 1: Understanding Your Child's Anxiety	5
Chapter 2: Signs and Symptoms of Anxiety	11
Chapter 3: Effects of Childhood Anxiety in Adulthood	23
Chapter 4: Caring for Socially Anxious Children	33
Chapter 5: Strategies to Support and Calm Your Child	45
Chapter 6: Five Phrases to Say to a Socially Anxious Child	57
Conclusion	67

Leaving a Review	69
About Author	71
References	73
More Books to Consider	75

Introduction

It was Heather's first day at school. We had been going over the details of today, but Heather was still hesitant to begin schooling. We had bought all of her crayons and drawing materials together. I let her personally pick out the type of bag she wanted. She wanted a cute pink bag with unicorn design, and she couldn't put it down all day. We also picked out her lunch box, pink again with fairies all over. She was all set for school. That morning, I woke up early to make her snacks. I packed her favorite Tuna sandwich, some breadsticks and an apple in her lunch bag. I even squeezed in a couple of chocolate bars. I woke Heather up and told her it was time to prepare for school. The look on her face was just one of utter horror. She just wanted to stay home. But the thought of using her pink bag eventually got her out of bed.

On the way to school, Heather was silent in the backseat. She was usually talkative during our car rides, but today, she kept on glancing at the windows, a look of apprehension deeply etched in her forehead. "Mom, can I start school next year?" she would ask me. "No, sweety, it's now or never." Heather wasn't too happy. Being the only child for some time, Heather was very attached to my husband and me. We were very hands-on in raising her. But growing up, we noticed that she was very sensitive to a lot of things. I actually talked about her in my previous book, "The Empathic Parent's Guide to Raising a Highly Sensitive Child: Parenting Strategies I Learned to Understand and Nurture My Child's Gift." Heather was a highly sensitive child, with a lot of special needs. But we adored her very much.

And now, school was becoming a problem for her. We arrived at the school and I wanted to just drop her and go. I needed to be at the office by 9 and I was already running late. I escorted her to the building and we admired the cool designs of the classrooms. Her room was at the far end. It was beautifully decorated with a lot of zoo animals. Her teacher, Mrs. Richards, was a kind looking lady and immediately welcomed Heather. I thought it would be ok because Heather had let herself be led to her chair. I was already walking away when I heard Heather throwing a tantrum. "I want my Mom!" She was making a scene and the other children were starting to get tearful. I had to go back to the classroom to reassure her. But

Heather just clung on to me. Mrs. Richards allowed me to stay for a while and enjoy the lesson with Heather. I was late, and I was stuck with my child who was mortally afraid of being left alone.

This scene may be very familiar to most parents. The first day at school is the most traumatic, as children are first exposed to a setting outside of home. I thought that the first day jitters were normal and would go away. But as the weeks went by, Heather still didn't let up her tantrums. Other children were already doing well in the classroom, making friends with each other. But Heather was still clinging on to me. After finding out about the highly sensitive person, I realized then that perhaps, she had a problem related to her high sensitivity. I researched, read a lot of books and talked to professionals. It was only then that I realized that my daughter was suffering from separation and social anxiety.

In this book, we will tackle the specific concern of separation and social anxiety, especially for kids who may be extremely shy and worried. I want to share my insights on raising a child with social anxiety to other parents who may be lost at what to do. The more that we know about our children's condition, the more that we will be able to respond best to their needs.

Chapter 1

Understanding Your Child's Anxiety

Each child we encounter will always be unique and incomparable. You may have four children and they could all be very different from each other. They have their own interests, likes, and dislikes, gifts and vulnerabilities, thoughts and feelings. Though they may share certain qualities, they cannot be truly comparable. Even the most identical of twins will have some amount of difference from each other. Being a kid yourself, you may have felt bad about being compared to your siblings as you state your own independence. And now that you have your own, it is good to first establish this uniqueness in every child. We can talk about them through certain similarities they have with others, but we cannot completely generalize their behavior.

And in dealing with stress, children will have different reactions. Some children thrive on it, seeing every problem as a challenge they can overcome. You may have experienced some children who are more daring than others, pushing the boundaries of social norms to state their own independence. These children can endure different problems from family and school and still come out strong. Some children may be slow to warm up. These children may be quite wary at first of an impending threat. But after gauging the safety of the environment, they are able to play and wrestle with the unknown. They may watch others first to see if the scene is safe and then proceed to play with others. And there are those with a low tolerance to stress. These are children who may be easily agitated or fearful when a problem comes up. Even at the slightest threat, they easily retreat to a safe zone or else tear up completely. Again, we have to say that children are unique and will respond to stress in different ways.

What then makes a child shy or anxious? There are several theories why some children are shyer than others. One perspective on shyness points out at a combined hereditary and social-upbringing factors as a cause. A child's disposition is usually inherited from their parents. The temperament of both parents or one of them can rub off on your child. If a mother is usually outgoing, has a lot of friends, goes out a lot, then the child has a higher chance of also being as outgoing. If the father is quite reserved and pensive, preferring to stay at home most of the time, then the child could also grow up as introverted. There are, of course, exemptions to this rule, but more or less, you can judge a fruit by its tree.

Second, modeling plays an important role in the process of socialization. Children always look up to their parents for everything, from the provision of food to being protected in a house and for their every other need. They look at their parents and try to mimic or copy their actions, thinking that it is what is right. The process of modeling works through observation and application. The child first observes the parent perform an action, and then tries it out for himself. When a mother says "Mama", the child will try to mouth "Mama." When a father blurts out a curse word, the child will also say the same, without regard if it's right or wrong. What the parents do, the child will also do. This modeling works to help children be eased into their social roles. A father demonstrates to his son how to ride a bike, play basketball, or tinker with a car. A mother shows her daughter how to sew a quilt, how to bake a cake, how to dress up for occasions. Shyness can then be seen as a product of a modeling scheme. When the parents try to avoid public places, the child will sense that this might be the right action and will mimic or do the same. If the parents are too worried to get out of the house, then the child will also imbibe that action as their own. This is not deterministic, as there are still some children who will develop their own behavior. But modeling is a strong explanation for shyness.

A third explanation for shyness points out a traumatic perspective of socialization. One negative event may have been imprinted on a child that he has generalized it to other situations. For example, a child may have encountered a stranger in a park while playing. The child may be initially friendly to the new child, even offering his toys. But the stranger may have hurt your child or stole his toys away. That memory may have stayed with your child. He was scared and hurt when he was trying to play with a stranger. In his mind, therefore, all strangers are not to be trusted. Negative events may have a stronger impact than positive ones. If we are not able to process these feelings, the child may nurture them for a long time and may convert that into extreme shyness and social anxiety.

There is no one formula to explain shyness and social anxiety. Different factors may be at work in the development of these behaviors. But we still have to deal with our children's anxiety. Yes, there are cases where the shyness is quite tolerable and we just have to let our children be. But sometimes, shyness can get in the way of your child's development. Because of social anxiety, your child may be afraid to go to school and that would compromise his education. Because of shyness, your child may need you to stay in the house at the expense of your work or your other errands. Then you create a problem of your own. It is imperative then to go to the root of the problem. We have to understand where the anxiety is coming from. If we want our children to develop well and to socialize confidently, then we must try to understand the anxiety behind the behavior.

Chapter 2

Signs and Symptoms of Anxiety

All of us experience some form of stress in our daily lives. Living in an imperfect world and interacting with different people, we are always prone and exposed to different kinds of stress. The intensity of stress will also vary according to the problem of each person. No two people will react to the same stress in the same way. Two students trying to answer the same Math problem in a test will have a different reaction to the stress. If one is more prepared, then there is less stress. But if the other has not really studied at all, then the stress level is greater. From simple morning traffic to the hassle of a long line, to more complicated problems like deciding to divorce your partner or experiencing death in the family, we all have our own experience and reaction to stress.

The Diagnostic and Statistical Manual of Mental Disorders V, states that anxiety is the anticipation of future threats. When we are faced with an impending stressful event, we experience anxiety. We may just be even thinking about a future event, and we are already anxious. On the one hand, anxiety helps us prepare better for the future. Because we are so concerned about an exam, we can prepare for it earlier by studying hard. When we are anxious about a business presentation, we review our material thoroughly beforehand. But on the other hand, anxiety can overwhelm us. Too much worrying can prevent us from doing our daily functions. Because we are so caught up worrying about getting sick, we don't go out of the house anymore. You are so anxious about speaking in public that you end up passing that opportunity for others to benefit from.

If there is such a thing as 'healthy' stress, the kind that helps us perform better, there is also such a thing as 'healthy' anxiety. But if the anxiety becomes pathological, then it will already affect our daily functioning. For a behavior or a thinking process to be pathological, two things are considered: the effect of the behavior on daily functioning and the duration of the behavior or thinking. One, we look at how anxiety prevents us from doing our daily functions. If too much worrying already prevents you from going to school or performing at work, then it is pathological. When the worry makes us miss family occasions or makes us neglect our health, then it is pathological. Second, the time duration is important. We will discuss different kinds of anxieties across the developmental age. The diagnoses of these conditions are only made when the behavior is evident for particular periods. Some diagnoses require the conditions to be present for at least 6 weeks, some for 6 months. The point is that the anxiety must exist for a prolonged period. We recognize that we can be anxious. But if we experience it unceasingly for more than a month, then we may have a problem.

Children too, experience all sorts of stress. Their concerns are totally diffcrent from adults', but the impact on their development is more profound. Children are just discovering their world and are entirely dependent on their parents. When they feel safe and secure with their family, they will seek to keep it that way. When they find their environment hostile, they will go back to the comfort of their family. They will start to meet other people aside from their family and that can be a difficult process of socializing. They will start to discover life outside their homes and for some that can be quite traumatic.

It is more difficult to diagnose anxiety disorders among children because most parents don't think of seeking help early. Some parents observe their children for long periods of time, hoping that their social anxiety will simply disappear. They keep on pushing their children into situations that they are not comfortable with, in the hopes that they will get over their own anxieties. It may work for some, but others will have bad memories of the experience. Some children will swim on their own if they are thrown into a pool, while some will drown out. And so, children never get the help they need at that stage. They will carry that childhood trauma later on into their adulthood, making them less functional.

I would just like to discuss in a particular way, the case of highly sensitive children (HSC). I have discussed this thoroughly in my previous book, but I feel the need to highlight their case in this instance. HSC feels anxiety much more intensely than other children. In terms of social circumstances, HSC will be more sensitive to the different sights, sounds, smells, tastes, and environment. They may not react to unfamiliar situations very well. It may take a while for them to warm up to others when they feel comfortable. It is important to understand how anxiety affects HSC because they are more sensitive to stress. You would need to guide them more carefully to become more resilient. Now, we are going to go over some disorders of anxieties children might experience.

Separation Anxiety Disorder

This disorder is seen mostly in children who are afraid of being separated from their parents and caregivers. A child is diagnosed with a separation anxiety disorder when he or she experiences at least three of the following symptoms:

Recurrent excessive distress when experiencing or anticipating separation from home

You will see these children really distressed when at the thought of leaving either one or both parents, depending on how attached they are to each other. They may cling on to them when they go out of the house, physically using their bodies to prevent you from exiting. Even just the thought of being actually separated makes them feel anxious already. We see this very commonly during the first day of school. There are some children who need their parents in the classroom for the first few weeks. They will cry and launch into a tantrum when their parents leave them. Eventually, some of them outgrow this and become comfortable with the school. But there are children who will still cry for their parents even after months of being in school. The separation just makes them more anxious.

Persistent worry about experiencing an untoward event that will cause separation from attachment figures

These children worry about different negative events that may happen to their parents. They are afraid that they will become sick and require them to be hospitalized away from home. Children feel that even cough and cold may warrant a trip to the hospital where they cannot go. They are anxious that their parents may meet with an accident on the road. They may sit in the car and are horrified at daydreams of experiencing an accident. They are mortified at the thought of losing their parents permanently. The thought preoccupies them and they need to see that their parents are physically ok before they can relax.

Reluctance to go out because of fear of separation

Going out of the house can be a daunting task for these children. Even the thought of going out the door mortifies them. Beyond the door, they feel very unsafe. They may consider the street and the neighborhood as foreign places. Parks, markets, schools, restaurants, and other public places scare them very much. They feel that the environment that is not their home is all dangerous places. Perhaps, they may have bad memories of these spaces, so they generalize it to other places. Because of the previous trauma, they are afraid of going out of the house.

Persistent fear of being alone without attachment figures

Socializing will be very hard for these children. They may always need the presence of their parents when they are interacting with other people. In family gatherings, for example, they may also be at the back of their mothers, trotting always behind her. When left to themselves, or with other people, they already feel anxious. They will keep looking at the crowd, trying to see if their parents are there. Failure to locate them will result in a meltdown.

Friendships in school are also problematic. They are not family and so these classmates will become strangers to them. They may not be able to participate in group activities because they will always want to be with their parents. This may often be a cause for bullying as they are termed "mama's boy or girl" or "papa's boy or girl".

Persistent nightmares involving separation

Children may wake up in the middle of the night, having dreamt of being separated from their parents. They will have no control over the content of their dreams, but because of excessive fear and anxiety, they carry that over to their dreams. That is why most of these children sleep with their parents in the same bed and room even if they are old enough to have their own. They need to have the physical security of being with their parents during sleep. This might cause problems when one parent has to leave for some legitimate reason. The child then may not be able to sleep well because of the separation.

Physical symptoms

When entertaining thoughts of separation, or having the actual experience of separating, these children will feel all sorts of physical symptoms such as nausea, vomiting, indigestion, palpitations, and difficulty of breathing. Some of these reactions may escalate to an exaggerated level that necessitates a trip to the hospital. The physical reaction is also their way of making you follow their wishes and address their concerns.

Selective Mutism

At home, you may observe that your child is able to converse well with you and with other familiar figures. They have a good vocabulary and they are able to express themselves well. Among their friends, they are also able to speak well. They can trade jokes, share stories and speak about their experiences. Intellectual competency may also be normal. They may do well in school in terms of written exams. But when these children are tasked to speak in front of the class, they suddenly become mute. There is selective mutism at work when children fail to speak in specific social occasions where they are expected to speak. Perhaps, they are afraid of being judged for how they speak or what they are speaking about. They are afraid of being ridiculed and embarrassed. So, they simply shut up.

But when the speaking occasion passes, they are able to speak normally. You may need to assess with a professional when you notice that your child is selectively being mute.

Specific Phobias

We say that anxiety is felt when anticipating a future threat. Fear is specifically felt when you are stressed about a particular object or situation. This specificity is called a phobia. Some people are afraid of spiders and we call that arachnophobia. Some people are afraid of crowded places and we call that agoraphobia. Your child might have a particular object or situation where he or she is afraid of. In other circumstances, they function normally. But when faced with that specific trigger, they launch onto hysterical cries and palpitations. They want to avoid that stimulus as much as possible. Try to observe what specific object your child may be afraid of.

Social Anxiety Disorder

We say that a child has social anxiety disorder when there is marked fear or anxiety in being in a social situation where there is possible scrutiny from others.

These will include social interactions such as conversations with strangers, eating out in public, commuting, shopping, or just walking in a crowded area. They fear occasions when they need to perform in public such as a recitation, a play, or a choir. Such situations are really frightening, but for socially anxious children, they may experience these more intensely. They may react to it even in an exaggerated manner including crying, throwing a tantrum, freezing, clinging to their parents, shrinking o,r failing to speak up. They will try to avoid these situations as much as they can. They would rather stay at home than visit a mall. They may volunteer others for recitation instead of taking the opportunity. They may delay work just to avoid social interactions. They are not able to function well when they are forced into social situations they have no control of.

With all these symptoms of anxiety, it is important to determine the extent of the condition in your child. Are they exhibiting anxiety symptoms only to a particular object or situation? Are they ok in general but clam up on social occasions? How does the anxiety manifest? Is schoolwork compromised? Have the symptoms been felt for a long time? These are questions you need to answer when you make an assessment of anxiety disorder. You may need to refer to a professional to help you spot these symptoms and address them earlier.

Chapter 3

Effects of Childhood Anxiety in Adulthood

You may feel hassled now taking care of your children. And you might think that they can outgrow all of that on their own. Some parents are experimental and would rather have their children exposed to so many stresses until they are able to overcome them. Yes, there are exceptions, where some children are able to move out of their social anxiety. But most of them will have traumatic experiences of standing in front of a crowd, being in a public and open space, and commuting using public transportation. Instead of learning from their mistakes, these children will remember those memories as bad reminders of their own incapability. Some of these children are often introverted and may not open up easily. As such, the repressed memories may persist through adulthood and affect their development. This chapter presents some of the dangers when childhood anxiety persists and is not addressed. Without proper recognition of the problem and adequate response, your child may develop some of these problems in adulthood.

Function Impairment

The trauma that they felt during childhood may affect different aspects of social functioning. One, their school performance may be compromised because of bullying and repeated exposure to stress. In fact, these children may be so traumatized to go to school that they end up staying at home. Their academic learning is stunted because they are afraid of other people bullying them or the prospect of doing something in front of other people where they can be embarrassed. If they continue to go to school, their attention may be drawn more towards avoiding other people or social exchanges rather than on the subject matter. They may be actually good in Sciences or Math, but because they need to work in groups or that they need to recite in front of everybody, their fear takes over learning. Hence, their potential is diminished, rendering them less than optimal when they are already working.

Second, the social relationships they build may also be compromised. If they are not able to establish friendships or even good communication and social skills at an early age, then they will find it difficult to work with other people. They may instead gravitate towards jobs that are solitary and afford minimal interaction with people. But if they don't practice relating to others, it may be difficult for them to cooperate and negotiate with others. They may be brilliant on their own, but when they are communicating their ideas to others, they may be lost in translation. The work is compromised when they need to work with other colleagues.

In terms of intimate relationships, it is still possible for them to be able to date and find life-long partners. But the process would be very difficult. They will have problems trusting other people because they have bad childhood experiences of relating to peers. Perhaps, they are going to look for other people who may resemble their attachment figures or someone who is as recluse as them. It will take a while before they can find their own friends and partners on their own. In terms of parenting, they may be the types who worry a lot, and that can translate to their unique parenting style. If they are not able to overcome the shyness and worry, they can easily transmit those characteristics to their children.

Medical Conditions

Social anxiety may also lead to certain physical symptoms. When you have a panic attack, you may have difficulty breathing, palpitations, headaches, nausea, and vomiting. There is less oxygen flowing inside of you and you will feel all sorts of pain. These are just acute symptoms related to stressful events. You feel these just as you are going out of the house or entering a public place. Usually, it would subside once the stressor has been eliminated. But for some, these reactions persist. When the conditions become chronic, you are prone to develop certain diseases.

With elevated blood pressure and palpitations, you may develop hypertension or other cardiovascular diseases. Stress actually releases certain hormones in the body that activate the body's fight or flight mechanism. When these chemicals persist beyond the required time, they can actually damage your blood vessels and organs. They may create harmful toxins that build up in your blood vessels, impeding blood flow. Thus, you develop hypertension. If you don't watch it, you are prone to clogging up vessels in your heart or in your brain leading to a heart attack or stroke. Do not disregard stress because it can actually contribute to the development of cardiovascular diseases.

Related to hypertension is obesity. When your kids stay home most of the time because they are afraid of the outside environment, the tendency for them is to eat and just sleep at home. Without much stimulus from the outside, they are going to be eating a lot of food, also to cope up with the stress that they feel. Sure, it may be negligible in childhood or even adolescence. But these bad eating patterns and sedentary lifestyles may induce your child to develop dyslipidemia or hypercholesterolemia. These are conditions where the excess fats consumed are stored in blood vessels. Over time, the fats will clog the vessels completely and compromise oxygen delivery. These may easily develop into other morbid diseases related to the cardiovascular system. Obesity will also make them less mobile. You also need to watch out for Diabetes Mellitus because of the junk food and sweets they consume. All of these will take a toll on your child when they become adults.

Mental Illness

Social anxiety will also predispose the individual to develop other mental disorders. The anxiety they feel may trigger other mental diseases when they are not addressed. We may not even be sure if the anxiety is the trigger or if it is a result of a pre-existing condition. But an individual with anxiety may have other mental conditions occurring at the same time. It is important for you to notice all the symptoms of mental diseases because negative consequences may occur.

One, individuals with social anxiety may develop depression. It is said that these two conditions, depression and anxiety, feed off each other. Because of the anxiety, you try to avoid people and the stressful environment. However, the isolation may also cause you to be depressed. In depression, you may have recurring negative thoughts about yourself, about the world and about the future. You may think that you are bad because you cannot relate well with others. For you, the world may be a toxic place filled with people who are out there waiting to embarrass you. And this cycle will just continue. Because of the depression, your sleeping and eating patterns will be heavily influenced, either in excess or in deficiency. The stress may cause you to overeat or to sleep less. You may feel tired most of the time. Your child will tend to withdraw to their safe zone and shield themselves from the world. They can just retreat into themselves and shut people out. When they do, it is hard to draw them back to normal functioning. The meltdown may take days and they may feel very depressed. Professional help may be warranted at this point.

Second, you really want to watch out for suicidal ideation and attempts from people with anxiety and depressive symptoms. We can see this among adolescents and young adults who are still in the process of managing their emotions. They have a lot of stress around them that they cannot fully process. It is good if they tell you these ideations because it means that they are open to being helped. But when they are shutting themselves from everyone, it is more difficult to help them. They are prone to suicide because they may just want to end the stress and the suffering they feel inside. They may think that they are worthless and blame themselves for everything. The sense of hopelessness pervades deep in them and the only escape is through suicide. Do not disregard any thoughts and verbal communication about suicide. Treat it as real and talk to your child. Do not wait until it is too late.

Lastly, having anxiety attacks may actually develop into personality disorders. The constant fear and anxiety may become more permanent and be the default way a person relates with others. With a sustained fear of others, a paranoid personality may be formed. This is where a person begins to mistrust everybody even without a good basis. They feel as if people are out to get them, plotting against them and talking behind their backs. They feel attacked most of the time even if in reality, that is not true. A dependent personality can also develop. This personality needs another person to function well. In their childhood, these children are highly dependent on their mothers and fathers. In adulthood, they will try to find mother and father figures that they can cling to. They cannot survive by themselves and need to depend on another person for their emotional needs. And an antisocial personality disorder can also develop. This would refer to a constant avoidance of all human contact. They want to be just by themselves most of the time, limiting all interactions with others. They will avoid circumstances that they will need to relate with other people. There are a lot more personality disorders that can develop when social anxicty persists. In all these, professional help may be warranted. So, try to detect signs of social anxiety early on to prevent other mental disorders from developing.

Chapter 4

Caring for Socially Anxious Children

It is not easy handling socially anxious children. Because of their particular needs, you would have to make a lot of adjustments. If it is your first time handling such children, you may feel overwhelmed and lost at what to do. As parents, we want the best for our children. We want to make them feel loved and supported. Seeing these children shy away from others may bother us. So many questions about how to raise them up or if the condition can be outgrown will pop into your mind. And all of this is normal. But now that you are able to recognize your child as having a heightened sensitivity, it is good to observe several guidelines when handling them. Unlike other children, you will need to exert extra effort to reach out to them. Here are some basic guidelines to help you care for socially anxious children.

Accept That They Are Children

First and foremost, remember that you are dealing with a child, not an adult. If you think that they can just outgrow their social anxiety on their own, you would be grossly mistaken. You might even be tempted to leave them alone in places out of frustration at their clinginess. This is terribly traumatic for them and will do them more harm. When you treat your children as adults, you are raising too high expectations of them. This will lead to more frustration for both of you. The child will try to please you by overcoming their fears to no avail and repeated failure while you will blame yourself for not raising your child well.

As children, they will need a lot of time and guidance to learn how things should be done. They are still developing and will be looking up to you for guidance. They will make a lot of mistakes. No matter how much you tell them that they shouldn't fear school or that it is safe crossing the street, they will still forget it and hold on tightly to you. Remember that they are very vulnerable at this stage. They are in the process of developing physically, mentally, emotionally, and socially. From the school-age years, they are going to discovering their talents and abilities, their limitations, and their capacities. They are still trying to find a way to fit in with others, constantly navigating the treacherous waters of socialization. They need friends but they might not know how. So, don't expect them to learn at the pace you want them to. They are kids still and will need some time to become confident and secure on their own.

But as children, their great advantage is really their eagerness to learn. They are curious about the world. But perhaps their fears and anxieties become so overwhelming that it paralyzes them. But if that fear and anxiety are addressed, there is a child inside who wants to play and be accepted for who he or she is. Your child may just have particular ways of learning about the world. Perhaps he doesn't like crowds too much or he hates noise. But children are very much willing to learn and discover the world. They have a thirst to know everything they could about the world. Perhaps other children are just more vocal about their intentions to learn, but yours is as curious. Capitalize on their childhood and their inexhaustible eagerness to learn, however peculiar their ways may be.

Highlight Their Giftedness

Before you can start complaining about how difficult it is to raise a socially anxious child, perhaps the first thing you should do is to find what is good with them. Many parents are so burdened that they may not realize just how good their children are despite their social awkwardness. They may simply focus on the hassle of raising a socially anxious child, on how annoying they can be when they cling on to you, or how difficult it is to send them to school. The frustration is understandable but let that not be the first and only thing that sticks to you when raising them up. Hard as it may be, find the good in each child and recognize that every one of them is gifted in their own way.

Even worry in itself may be a good characteristic, given it is in moderation. There is such a thing called 'good worry.' Because we care so much for something, we exert a lot of thought over making sure that everything is perfect for that event or person. When a child is showing signs of worry, it may also be that they are trying to be more careful. It could be a care for their own health and well-being. Their worry could be for you. They may want you to be safe and out of harm. In fact, because of the worry, you take extra precautions to be safe. In a way, this helps us second-check our decisions to make sure we are not making a mistake. The worry then is translated into productive anticipation of future events. Yes, that could easily be abused and exaggerated. But then again, not worrying at all could also be a red flag. A child who easily goes with strangers or does risky behaviors also puts himself in harm's way. It is actually more difficult to discipline a child who has his own mind rather than having one who is more on the careful side.

Social anxiety in children also masks their gift of obedience and listening. They are so fixated on you and will listen to your every word. As parents, you have to be grateful to have children who will listen to you and actually obey what you command them to. Discipline comes easy for these socially anxious children because their modeling instincts are still very intact. You can exploit this advantage by teaching them the values and habits you want them to learn. When they grow up, they will have a mind of their own. During childhood, you have a captive audience in your children. They are still malleable and trainable. Hence, our responsibility as parents to develop good morals in them is bigger during childhood. It may be grace then that they are still shy at this point.

And maybe, a little reassuring word may go a long way for these socially anxious children. We will discuss which power words to express to these children. But we need to empower them because most often, socially anxious children behave the way they do because they fail to see their giftedness. They may be good at drawing or Mathematics. They may excel in constructing intricate designs or manipulating tools. They may actually like reading and have a good vocabulary set. They may actually be good at teamwork or have leadership capabilities. But all of that disappears at the thought of performing in public or expressing those with gifts to other people. They fail to see beyond their fear and anxieties. As parents who can see the whole picture further, draw your child to see their giftedness also. Compliment them when they do a good job in school or at home. Display their artworks or hang their awards on a wall. Celebrate by eating out in their mini achievements. When socially anxious children are able to draw confidence from their achievement, they may be more secure to venture out of their shells. When they see that in other aspects they are doing well, they become more confident to share with others. Find your child's giftedness and use that as his strength.

One-step at a Time

As adults, we may be very used to multi-tasking. Once given a set of instructions, we have the ability to proceed on our own to accomplish the different tasks set before us. It is not uncommon to see people talking over their smartphones while typing on their laptops and squeezing a bite or two of lunch during pauses. We pride ourselves on being able to do many things at one time to show just how efficient we are. And it is very wrong for us to expect kids to be the same way. We cannot tell them to speed up on their tasks and make them do all sorts of activities all at the same time. They are not yet adults.

So, it is good to do things one step at a time. For example, your child may be very afraid of going to the market. It will be very traumatic for them if you just drag them over the grocery store and let them cry it out as you do your shopping. Instead of learning, they are simply overwhelmed by the anxiety and trauma you dealt them with. This is not a good way of teaching your kids. What you can do is a stepwise approach. Start by accompanying them to the door. Practice going in and out of the door until they are comfortable. Next, you can proceed with taking them across the street. It will be worrisome at first. So just gauge their level of comfort and then return to the house. The next day, try going to the other side. After a week, they can get used to crossing streets. Just inch your way day by day, week by week, until you are able to reach the market. It is tiresome and slow, but that is the only way they will learn.

Prepare Them to be Functional

What is good with children is that they are still in the process of becoming and learning. Unlike adults who are already set in their ways, children are still very much trainable. They can still adapt from their set ways given the proper instructions and modeling. It is actually exciting to teach children because their development is very dramatic. You can see day by day how they are able to move from mastery of one skill to the other. Today they start counting numbers from one to ten. The next week, they can already count up to 20. Before long, they can start adding simple numbers. And then, they will be able to subtract them. And so on. Socially anxious children are particularly enjoyable to teach because they pick up very fast. They are very focused on details and will obey you every step of the way. They like learning and when you start teaching them, they will absorb everything you say like a sponge.

Knowing this, we can say that it is possible to help your children outgrow social anxiety. They are still in the stage of learning and it is possible to learn how to socialize well. It must be clear to you that having them develop social skills is essential to their growth. You cannot just tolerate every tantrum they have and give in all the time. Just because you love them does not mean you will baby them forever. On the contrary, if you really love them, you should be firm in your ways to help them grow steadily from childhood to adolescence to adulthood in increasing maturity. They will need your help as children, but they cannot depend on you all their lives. You cannot be there for them all the time because you have a life of your own.

In order to do this, you must be able to play the roles of being a parent and a teacher for them. As a parent, you will endow them with unconditional love and support. As teachers, you should teach them by challenging them at an appropriate level. You should be able to balance supporting them as well as challenging them. You must be firm when you set rules for them. Don't tolerate tantrums as you would in any child. They will cry, but afterward, explain to them how their actions have consequences in real life. If they refuse to go to school, try curtailing some of their privileges like watching TV or playing with their toys. Explain to them the values of learning that they miss out on when they don't go to school. Teach them values in a way that they will learn from their mistakes. It is tedious, but it is the only way they will be prepared for life.

Family Is the Key

You don't need to do it alone. You may think that the burden of teaching and raising your child belongs solely to you. The impulse to shoulder everything is felt more intensely by single parents raising their children on their own. When you have this lone wolf mindset, you will easily get tired. When you start taking care of your children on your own, the tasks may even overwhelm you. Socially anxious children will have their particular quirks and needs that you will need to attend to. But you are not just a parent. You still have to do well at work and earn an income. At night, you may feel so tired but you still have to cook or check on your child's work. When your child has social anxiety problems, the burden becomes heavier. At some point, you may even be burnt out and may start lashing on your child unintentionally.

It doesn't have to be this way. If you are not a single parent, then you have your partner to rely on. If you have other children, it is the task of everyone to take care of each other. As parents, you take the lead in setting good examples for your children. But the other siblings can also teach their brothers and sisters. Make them feel responsible for each other. Share the burden with your partner. It is not a good practice to have someone focus on earning the income alone and letting the other deal with the children. You are both responsible for raising your children and not just putting money and food on the table. Strengthen teamwork and the load will be much more bearable for all of you. Social anxiety in children may not be common and people will need to adjust to your child's condition. Involve everyone in dealing with this challenge.

Seek Professional Help

Know that there is always help when you need it. Some parents may feel that it is their sole responsibility to raise their kids. But let's face it, we don't know everything. There might come a point when we really don't understand our children anymore. Rather than just letting them be, it is good to seek professional help. It is a misnomer to think that psychologists are just for crazy people. On the contrary, we all need some form of help and these professionals may give us that objective guidance we need in raising our children.

In the case of social anxiety, there are a number of specialists who may be able to help you. Developmental pediatricians and psychiatrists may be the most equipped in helping you deal with your child's social anxiety. They have studied the condition for many years and have developed a lot of research in that field. They may also have come across many other children and have helped other parents deal with them. Don't be afraid to ask for help because these professionals are entirely at your service. They may be able to suggest to you therapies that you can enroll your child in. They may teach you ways to deal with difficult children. And they may just expand your perspective on dealing with social anxiety. It is perfectly ok to ask for help. The earlier you seek it, the faster the problem is solved.

Chapter 5

Strategies to Support and Calm Your Child

It is important that you adopt the perspectives discussed in the previous chapter. These will help you prepare well for the daily management of your child with anxiety. It is one thing to learn about taking care of your child, and another thing to actually do it. There may be times when you will feel hopeless and tired after not being able to understand them. These strategies will help you take care of your child better. It will be difficult at first, but once you get the hang of practicing these daily, you will develop routines that will come easy for you. In all these strategies, it is important to gauge your child's reactions to everything that you do. How you will proceed will depend very much on your child's openness and willingness to learn and to change his or her thinking and behavior. Go slow and exercise a lot of patience and your child will slowly react positively.

Find a Safe Zone

The very first thing you need to do is to determine the safe zone of your child. When your child becomes very anxious about a stressful event, they are highly likely to experience a panic attack. They may become so overwhelmed with emotions and fear that they cannot think much anymore and will just let themselves be inundated with their feelings. Their reaction can also be exaggerated. This can range from simple crying and tantrums, or difficulty to move. But at its worst, physical symptoms may even warrant a visit to the Emergency room. With panic attacks especially, there could be feelings of nausea, vomiting, and difficulty of breathing. A simple trigger may send your child into a panicked state.

Instead of also panicking, the very first thing you need to do is to calm down your child. When they are panicking, they have less oxygen circulating in their brain and body. You need to help them breathe deeper and slower. Make them inhale and exhale deeply so that more of the oxygen flow in and the poisonous carbon dioxide be eliminated. You will see that they will calm down once they get enough oxygen circulating.

Next, you have to identify a safe zone. What is a safe zone? This is an area or an environment where your child feels most comfortable and at ease. This is entirely dependent on your child's preference. They may feel safe in their own bedroom or anywhere inside the house. They may feel that they are safe when you hug them or when they are holding a particular toy. They may feel safe when they have their headphones playing their music. They may feel safe when there are no people and there is less noise. Whatever it is, you have to identify that environment. When they feel stressed, you must be able to return to that safe zone. You want to remove that stress by returning to a place of comfort. This will help you establish a baseline that you can always return to. Children need to feel secure, so you have to respect that space. Let them retreat to their safe zone when they feel stressed. When they are calmer, that is the time when you can process their thoughts and feelings. And when you want to attempt to change their behavior, it is important that you let them know that they can easily run to their safe zone.

Develop Routines and Then Expand Them

Socially anxious children are very protective of routines. They like things that are predictable where they know what will happen most of the time. They have a great need for control especially when they feel stressed. They may follow particular routines at home, a specific time for waking up and sleeping, for meals and activities. Their things may be arranged in a particular manner and they easily know when something is missing or placed improperly. When they are able to follow their routines, they feel very much at ease and distressed. Of course, when that routine is changed even to some degree, then they will feel a lot of stress.

In real life, we cannot stick to routines rigorously. Yes, there are certain patterns of behavior we may be comfortable with. But it cannot be followed all the time due to circumstances we cannot control. A certain amount of resilience is needed. You need to be able to teach that resilience to your children in a way that is appropriate and understandable for them. You have to respect their routines, but at the same time, challenge those routines to help them develop resilience.

Two components are needed for this strategy. First, we have already discussed the safe zone. Children must be able to return back to their safe zone, so they feel calm and protected. In the case of routines, going back to their routine is a source of safety for them. So, you have to establish their routine and respect that. If they want to do their homework in a particular way that works for them, respect that. If they want a certain order to your shopping routine, just go along with that. They need to know that they can easily return to their routine before you pose a challenge.

Next, when you want to change their routine, the degree of change must not be too drastic. It must be different from their routine, but not radically strange. For example, your child is comfortable only eating meals at home. You noticed that anywhere else, they would clam up and not touch the food. In order to change this behavior, you have to introduce incremental changes to their routine. First, eat together inside the house. Your child will feel safe with this arrangement. Next, try eating outside the main house but still within your home. It could be on the porch or on a bench near the door. The child will still feel safe because it is still near your home and that they can easily go inside. But you already exposed them to eating at a different place. Next, you can try eating at a nearby restaurant or a breakfast place. It must be near your home so that they can feel comfortable. Expand the distance from your home at each mealtime over weeks. Do it slowly so that your child will not notice the changes very much. After a while, they will feel comfortable eating at different places. If you change immediately from eating at home to eating out at a restaurant, they may feel anxious and stressed that they won't learn anymore. The next challenge for you is to help them eat out in a different place without your presence, for example at school. For this, just follow the incremental changes in routine.

The safe zone and incremental change will help your child to change his or her behavior in a safe and comfortable way. Do not traumatize your child by making big leaps in terms of routine change. You can develop resilience in a controlled way. Of course, you cannot maintain that atmosphere when they become adults. There are a lot of factors you cannot control anymore, and they would have to do it for themselves. But at least, you are able to help them develop resilience slowly but surely.

Be Good Models

There are many ways in which people learn. Some people learn by reading a manual and applying the concepts after. These people like to understand everything in their minds first before they can apply what they learn. Some people learn by doing. They may not have any idea on how the thing works but they will just tinker with it and learn on the spot. This happens in the case of biking where there is no other way to learn but to simply bike. We all have our own ways of learning. Children learn things in a different way. Unlike adults, they cannot read manuals, or their limbs may not be equipped to handle things. Infants and young children learn by modeling. Children will look at their attachment figures and will copy whatever they do.

Modeling first works through the process of attachment. Infants observe their mothers first. They receive nourishment and milk from them, so they feel very secure with their mothers. Because they receive sustenance and unconditional love from their mothers, they will feel much attached to them. They feel safe around their mothers. That attachment is then extended to their fathers and to other caregivers. Children observe that when they cry and the father addresses the problem, by changing their diapers or feeding them milk. When they feel safe with that caregiver, they will also form attachments. The degree of attachment is highly dependent on the consistency of the positive reinforcement. When the child cries, the mother or the father should be there to calm the child down. When they are consistently present, attachment is very strong. But when there are prolonged times when the child is left unattended, the attachment will be very poor. The child will think that he or she can depend on the parents consistently. They will develop a tentative attachment, but with a lot of mistrust.

As they grow up, children will also refer back to their attachment figures. They regard their father and mother as perfect and will try to emulate them. When their parents eat, they will also eat. If they use spoons and forks, they will use those too. If they use chopsticks, they will also use chopsticks. They will constantly look to their parents for validation of their actions. The attachment can also become very dependent when the children have to constantly refer back to their parents for everything. Social anxiety is exaggerated when they are not able to form independent choices for themselves.

Given such an arrangement, your job is to be a good model to your children. If they see that you are comfortable meeting strangers, then they will also try to feel comfortable around different people. If you are also wary and have few friends, preferring to stay at home, then they will also be very recluse. If you like to engage people in conversation, then your child will also feel comfortable speaking up. If you are the type to also be very introverted, then your child will also be one.

Hence, you have to be the model for your child. If you want to change their behavior, you have to do it first and they will follow. If your child is anxious about going to school, be with them physically in the first few weeks. You cannot expect them to learn on the spot. They will still need to verify the safety of the environment with you. And when they become comfortable enough, that is the time when you can slowly disengage. But you cannot leave them hanging at the first instance. You will need to model and hopefully, your children will learn gradually.

Coordinate With Schools

It is important for you to coordinate with the school regarding the special needs of your child. For some parents, they would rather home-school their own children or send them to special schools. This has its own pros and cons. But you can still send your child to normal schools provided that you maintain close coordination with the school. You are not asking the teachers to do special favors for your child when you coordinate. You want to explain the circumstances of your child so that the teachers can gauge the kind of learning process that will be optimal for your child and his peers. The school is the extension of the home, another place where children can learn. So, you have to get your teachers involved in the upbringing of your children.

You want to monitor especially your child's academic performance. The school setup can be a very anxious-filled environment. We have seen how some kids will clam up when they need to speak in front of a class. This can affect very much how they will fare in the different subjects. They may be excellent at the non-verbal parts of the lessons but may do poorly in public speaking. Your goal is not to stop the teachers from doing these activities. There is a good reason why this is done and this will actually benefit your child develop his speaking skills. Coordinate with the teachers so that the process of schooling is not as traumatic.

You also want to watch out for bullying. Socially anxious children are very much prone to bullying because they are different from their peers. Some children will find your child to be eccentric, a crybaby, a softy, or a mute weakling. Their heightened sensitivity may become the source of laughter of their classmates. Their academic performances may plummet as a result of this bullying. A lot of insecurity and anxiety are developed when the bullying is not addressed. What complicates the problem is that your child will not open up easily to you. They may try to resolve it on their own. You may only know of it when something really bad has happened. It is good that you coordinate with the school when bullying happens. When you feel that your child is being bullied, it is essential that you try to sort out their feelings. They need to feel safe with you to divulge their feelings of hurt and shame. Children need to vent out their repressed feelings or they might implode. The more that you are able to recognize signs of bullying, the earlier you can address the problem.

Chapter 6

Five Phrases to Say to a Socially Anxious Child

I truly believe in the power of words. We can say so many things that will affect people intensely. You can use words to hurt other people and to cause a lot of misunderstanding. When you gossip or slander somebody, your words are already hurting other people. But words can also uplift others. When you compliment them for the good things they do or you extend your concern to others, you are sharing a lot of positivity in the world. You can also use words to heal and nurture. In the case of your children, you have to be very careful with your choice of words. When dealing with socially anxious children, you have to remember that you are coming from an area of insecurity. The anxiety and fear are but a mask for the inadequacy they feel inside. As parents, your task is really to get them out of that area of insecurity to an area of confidence, from a position of weakness to a position of strength. If you want to support and change your child, then here are some key phrases you need to say repeatedly to them. The more that they hear these, the more they will be encouraged to be resilient in spite of their anxiety.

"It's ok"

When your child is experiencing a panic attack, you have to tell them "It's ok." These two words can easily calm your child down. Your words actually become a safe zone for them. When you say that "it's ok," you are taking the stress away from them and making the environment safe for them. Your words cushion the impact of stress on your child and he will calm down more easily. When you say these words, you should also be sure that the situation is indeed safe for them. They can relax their defenses and think more rationally when they feel that you are making the environment safe for them.

When you say, "it's ok", you are also acknowledging their feelings. They will feel that their anxiety and fear are not something they imagined but can be conquered. You are validating what they are feeling as true, but also these feelings are also manageable. This is important because there are words and actions that mean to disregard the feelings of your child. When you say to them, "Don't feel anxious, there is nothing to be afraid of," you are saying that what they are feeling is not true. But it is true for them. Recognize the fear and anxiety because that is what they are really feeling. But when you say "It's ok" you are also saying that that anxiety will also pass. Yes, it is there, but they can overcome it.

"You can do it"

You should be the number one cheerleader of your children. It is one thing to think that you are supporting your children, and another to actually say it and show it expressively. Children need to know that their parents approve of them. It might be tiresome for you, but children are in constant need of validation. They want to know if what they are doing is right and pleasing for you. Hence, do not be too stringent in making them feel appreciated. Because of their fear and anxiety, they may feel depressed and disheartened. Words like "You can do it" will uplift their spirits and enable them to keep on trying.

When you say that "You can do it", you are also affirming their giftedness. Because of a lot of bullying, they will be very insecure about their talents and skills. They feel so threatened by other people and by strange environments that they cannot see just how gifted they are. Their anxiety prevents them from expressing their talents. They may actually have good ideas, but because they are afraid to speak in public, they are seen as having weak minds. When you say, "You can do it," you are affirming their gifts and prodding them to share it with others. Instead of focusing on the things that they cannot do, try highlighting all the other things they do well. If they can draw beautifully, affirm that. When they are able to design complicated Lego buildings, celebrate that. When they are able to be confident in one thing, they will be able to be secure in other things. From one place of stability, they can move on to other aspects. They will need just one person who will believe in their giftedness.

"Try again"

When children fail to meet expectations, they are going to feel very down. They will try to please you and meet the goals that you want for them. But sometimes, their fears and anxieties get the best of them. Socially anxious children in particular brood over failure for a long time. They may feel that they are inadequate when they don't meet expectations. Their particular needs supersede their attempts at overcoming their social anxiety. Yes, they want to go to school. Yes, they want to meet new friends. Yes, they want to be able to play with other children and go to places on their own. But somehow, their social awkwardness prevents them from being as sociable as other people. They will try and fail. One time, a second time, a third time, they can be very prone to failure and rejection.

It is during these times that they would need your reassuring support and words. When you tell them "Try again", you are encouraging them to keep on trying. This builds up resilience in children when they know they can start anew each time they fall. More than the number of times that they fall, count the number of times they are willing to try again. It is ok to make mistakes. But it is essential that they try again and again until they succeed. With these words, you are setting the stage for them to become more confident in handling rejection and failure. When they don't meet expectations, it is not the end of the world. There is always a tomorrow where they can continually try. And the more that they try, the more that they will master and conquer their fears. Without these words, they will simply clam up and remain in the house, clinging on to you. But when you prod them to discover the world, they will slowly appreciate the value of trying again.

"I am here"

When you say, "I am here", you are reassuring your child that you are not separating from them and are just within striking distance. This is important when the child is trying to explore new territories. They have to have that assurance of the safe zone, the presence of their attachment figures. This is connected to modeling, wherein you have to be physically present when you enact certain changes in their routine. When you are there, your child will feel comfortable trying a different way of doing things, go a little further from the house, meet new people, and speak to strangers. Even just your physical presence already calms them. You want to tell "I am here" more frequently to them as a sort of mantra they can use even when you are not around. They have to inculcate in their minds that whatever they do, their parents will always be for them.

But you also have to mean this before you say it. You cannot assure them "I am here" when you are always busy doing something else. Of course, you have a life of your own and will need to do many other things aside from raising children. You still need to take care of your business and your work, relate with your colleagues and bosses. You have your own friends to catch up with. You and your husband should always have some time together. And of course, you will need to reserve time for yourself. This is all understandable. But make sure that you reassure your child with your presence in the moments they need you. It may not be always as you have a lot of other aspects to attend to. But in their growing years, try to be there for their milestones. Be there on their first day of school. Be there when they are celebrating school events. Be there when they need someone to talk to. Even if you are busy, spend time with your kids. Only then would "I am here" mean anything to them.

"Be yourself"

Finally, assure your children always that they are wonderful just as they are. Sure, they may be annoying at times. Sure, they may be whiny or prone to tantrums. But at the end of the day, they are still your children. They are beautiful because they come from someone as beautiful as you. It is just that these kids who are extremely shy or have social anxiety have to put up with a lot of fears and insecurity. They are afraid to show their talents and abilities to others. Their shyness prevents them from sharing their wonderful personality with others.

Be sensitive to this. Let your children feel that they can be themselves, whether in your presence or in others. Teach them to stand up to bullying. They may not need to be confrontational, but they have to stand their ground against bullies. You will be able to help them socialize better when you constantly assure them that they are likable just as they are. When you say, "Be yourself," you are celebrating both their giftedness and limitations. You are telling them that they are talented and beautiful just as they are. You are also affirming that they are still in the process of overcoming their shyness and social awkwardness. You are affirming that they are lovable just as they are. And that will go a long way. When children feel they are loved, the anxiety and the fear are kept at bay.

Conclusion

Having children is a blessing. Whoever they may be, whatever qualities they may possess, never forget that children are blessings. They are a fruit of love and you must shower them with love. They in turn will endow you with more love. There may be times that they are difficult to manage, especially when they throw tantrums and become inconsolable. There will be times when you are not at your best, when you feel tired and overworked. During these lows, try to remind yourself that these children are very precious. All of our work is dedicated really to making sure that these children are loved and will have the best chances at a good life.

And being blessings, each child will be different. They have their own temperaments and quirks. They have their own habits and tricks. Some of them will be extremely shy and worry a lot. Some of them may be afraid to speak in public. Some of your children may be afraid to be around strangers. They may have the best ideas, the most imaginative stories, the most precise scientific knowledge contained inside of them.

But because of their social awkwardness, that earth-shaking potential is locked in. The idea of performance or of social interaction dilutes or even completely obliterates that wonderful potential.

And to all these, be patient. Be patient with them until they are able to learn from their mistakes. Be patient as they try out different things at their own pace, however slow it may be. Be patient when they cannot overcome their fears instantly. And most of all, be patient with yourself. Of course, nobody expects you to be the perfect parent. You will have your own mistakes. You will snap sometimes out of frustration. You may lose your cool and insist on your own ways. Be patient with yourself and try again and again to be sensitive parents to your sensitive children. We all need a lot of patience to help us all grow together.

Leaving a Review

As an independent author with limited marketing resources, reviews for my books are essential in order to survive as an indie writer. New works of literature get published daily, so there's no guarantee that any given work will be successful.

Your review can help authors like me grow and share their knowledge with more people. If you enjoyed this book, I would really appreciate your honest feedback. You can leave a review by going to this book's page on Amazon, where it is listed, and clicking "Write A Review."

Leaving an honest review can also help other people find this book easily on Amazon and benefit from it as well. Your feedback is important to me so I can find out what you like and don't, which in turn helps me make better decisions about my writing style.

Thank you,

Freeda

About Author

Freeda is a bestselling author who has written multiple books on parenting and family life. She knows that raising children can be tough, but it's also one of the most rewarding experiences any parent can ever have. She has devoted her life to understanding the psychology behind good parenting and shares what she's learned with others through her books, blogs, and newsletters.

She is also a mother of a highly sensitive child. Freeda shares her story not just to help other parents learn how to raise a highly sensitive child but also to impart lessons on what helped her get through the challenges and live a happy life for both herself and her daughter.

After years of navigating the parenting journey herself, Freeda knows that sharing her life experiences with others could help them on their own parenting journeys. She has helped countless mothers, fathers, grandparents, babysitters, and teachers in making their lives easier by providing sound advice from her extensive experience with children's behavior patterns over the years.

In her free time, she goes to her Yoga and Pilates classes. She also loves baking, especially when requested by her children. Their favorite is her bunch of chewy white chocolate macadamia cookies.

Check out Freeda's profile on Amazon: https://www.amazon.com/author/freedameighan

References

American Psychiatric Association. (2013). Diagnostic and statistical manual of mental disorders (DSM-5®). American Psychiatric Pub.

More Books to Consider

Also available in Audiobook format

My good friend, Grace, wrote these books. Please check them out too.

Printed in Great Britain
by Amazon